This is Real Talk

Connecting With Young People By Saying What Needs to be Heard

Adolph Brown

CreateSpace
4900 LaCross Road
North Charleston, SC 29406
USA

This is Real Talk
Connecting With Young People By Saying What Needs to be Heard
Copyright © 2008 by Adolph Brown

CreateSpace books may be ordered through booksellers or by contacting:

CreateSpace
4900 LaCross Road
North Charleston, SC 29406
USA

ISBN: 978-1543054255
ISBN: 1543054250

Printed in the United States of America

PRAISE FOR DR.BROWN:

"Doc is hip and his spirit is sincere as he shares personal stories of his humble beginnings. Many of us experienced personal breakthroughs. You have an ability to have an instant connection to others. You are my Humble Hero!" --Nelson Angier, Emory University

"The talk you gave was simply the most uplifting I have ever heard, many people personally found me to tell me that it was a marvelous keynote address to round off our day."--Jeremy Ryder, Andersen Consulting

"Your story is not only about the human spirit, it was really about all of us." --Cheryl Townsend Bunting, Parent Involvement Specialist

"People who were previously unhappy and disenfranchised were empowered, charged for positive action, and began taking responsibility for the success of the organization. He brought experience, heart, and wisdom to our division." --Chad McCaskill, Camden County Public School System

"I needed new ways to connect with my students. You re-ignited my passion to educate. Your disarmingly composed manner provides a great role model for teaching excellence." --Hope Mitchell, Long Beach, California

"Top tier speaker and trainer. Adolph didn't get voted best in the business by being boring. He is equally kind as he is funny." --Randolph Johnson, Speak 4 Life

"Dr. Adolph Brown has his scars and his stars. To hear him speak and feel it too is awesome. He is indeed an Ambassador of Hope."--Rev. Jesse Jackson, Rainbow Push Coalition

"You have the gifts to change the hearts and minds of skeptical people...He definitely understands the issues and provides practical strategies to work on them...A MUST for ALL school divisions!" --Dr. Fred Bateman, The Urban Superintendents Conference of America, Charleston, South Carolina

"You are truly a jet-setter. You wooed us with your optimism, knowledge, and empathy. Thank you for guiding us to more self-awareness and appreciation. You created a ripple effect of teamwork and increased productivity in our organization." --Nippon Hiroshi, Tokyo, Japan

"Doc Brown is an inspiring, excellent, and enthusiastic scholar." –Pamela Woods, Brookline, MA

"Adolph speaks from the heart and is a truly gifted motivational speaker. His talks become the highlight of every event." --Raymond Osbourne, National Counselor's Association

"Doc is one sharp guy! Keep motivating with the humor, honesty and wisdom. Information shared by humor is retained. We love him." --Susan Teri, Rotary International

"You were fast-paced, upbeat, and INCREDIBLY funny. Thanks for the exuberant spirit and laughter. You are a special person." --Fred Reid, World Racing Teams and Motorsports, Tennessee

"One-of-a kind presenter! Fabulously off the charts. We had an amazing meeting due in part to your high energy, knowledge base, and enthusiasm coupled with positive audience interaction. Thanks for coming and leaving the positive attitude with us!" --Cordia Stinebaugh, Burger King Corporation

"As teachers we must not forget as Doc says that 'relationships yield results' and 'the tree is in the seed.' Children come to us with great possibilities and we must make those dreams and possibilities become a reality by accepting all children [to ride in our wheelbarrows]... all educators should be afforded the opportunity to hear and work with you." --James Thornton, Division Superintendent, Cumberland County Public Schools

Dedicated to

All of the instructors, trainers, and supervisors I have studied with over the past 25 years.

Terry Morawski (aka "TMo") has given me considerable time and energy that has been invaluable in completing this book.

Thanks to my reviewers: Mrs. Susan Tolley, Mrs. Marla Brown, and Dr. Gregory Pierce, M.D.

The countless interactions in the classroom have given me endless opportunities to learn and evolve as a Master Teacher. I am deeply indebted to all the students I have either personally taught or lectured throughout my travels for sharing so much of themselves and being involved in the process of personal growth and exploration.

I thank my mother, Virginia Brown, and Great-aunt, Lorraine Moore, who always encouraged me to be a free spirit (within reason) and taught me the importance of education and continued learning. I thank my grandfather who gave me unconditional love.

Most of all, my greatest heartfelt appreciation goes to my wife, Marla, and family. You guys are and will continue to be my greatest teachers and inspiration. Thank you for insisting that I practice what I teach and for giving me plenty of opportunities to do so.

Contents

Foreword

I got so tickled. Adolph allowed me to read his book while it was in draft form. In the draft on the Foreword page, it was written in "Expert Educator to Write." Then Adolph asked me to write it. While I am an educator, I am not an expert. I was Adolph's third grade teacher. Either lots of experts turned him down or he still sees me through the eyes of an eight-year-old. I suspect the latter.

Truth be told, in many ways I still see Adolph as a child no matter how he has grown, no matter the multitude of achievements in his life, no matter the accolades he has received. I feel a great deal of pride in his accomplishments, and I feel protective of him much the same as I felt thirty years ago.

I am not, however, surprised what a fine man Adolph is nor am I surprised at his achievements. Adolph grew up in the projects. He lived in an area where ambulances didn't go in without a police escort. After dark, the streets were frightening places. That mattered little to Adolph or more importantly to Adolph's mother, Mrs. Virginia Brown. Mrs. Brown raised her children in a home rich in many ways. Her children were raised in a home rich in caring. Mrs. Brown cared deeply about people - about her family, about her neighbors, and about those of us fortunate to cross her path. Her children learned these lessons from her. Adolph was a kind, empathetic child; don't confuse that with a "pushover" because he was known to use his fists upon occasion. But he was thoughtful and always a good listener. He, like his mother, genuinely cared about people.

He was also raised in a home rich in the belief that education mattered and it was valued. Adolph wasn't an all "A" student back in 3rd grade, but he wasn't far off. Adolph wanted to succeed; he wanted to learn. But there's a part of me that always believed he did not want to bring home a paper on which he had not tried his hardest.

Finally, Adolph was raised in a home rich in the value of giving of oneself. Mrs. Brown would do anything for anyone.

I've seen her cater a full meal for one of Adolph's college classes. Adolph, too, will put himself out for someone else. I must admit at a younger age, he did need some guidance in that department. Once, when he was in fifth grade, he saw me escort a recalcitrant student to the office. Later that day, Adolph knocked on my door and asked me if I wanted him to "take that boy out" after school. While the offer was somewhat tempting, I told Adolph firmly "No!" Even the nice need direction.

This is the Adolph that I know. I am so proud (and, yes, protective) of him. I still learn from him and will always love him, as I do so many of my former students including ViVi Adolph's sister. (But that's a whole other book!)

Thank you, Adolph for being such a wonderful student and a wonderful teacher. Enjoy Adolph's *This Is Real Talk*. It is written by real good man.

Susan K. Tolley

Introduction

First, thanks for picking up this book. I don't think you will be disappointed. I've got years of experience and miles of heart invested in this project. And I'm a strong believer that everything happens for a reason, so the fact that you picked up this book is no accident.

I've got quite a bit to share with you. We'll have a few laughs, maybe a few tears, plenty of "aha" moments, and more; before we get started, I want to share a story with you that I think will explain where I'm coming from.

I grew up in the notorious Bayside Arms Projects, or "BAP," where it was not uncommon to step over a person in the street in the morning on the way to school and then step over that same person at the end of the day on the way home. I was often the "stinky" child in class because our family's water had been turned off. I was the child who was disruptive in class. In other words, I know about troubled kids because I was one, but I learned early that my success in life was up to me.

The teachings of my mother and some other select adults cut through the negativity of the streets, the gangs, the drugs, etc., that were all around me. I learned to live by what has now become one of my favorite messages - "Wanna be; gonna be." I know that no amount of background issues create a good excuse for failure and despair. I had all the makings of a criminal, but I channeled that energy into something positive. As I tell kids every day, "It's not what they call you, it's what you answer to, and now people call me **Doctor Brown**."

This is Real Talk is the reflective opinion of everyday ordinary people. These reflections are sound and prudent and somewhat unsophisticated. It is critical thinking at the most basic of levels—behavior that should be automatic. So said, we must dialogue with young people to understand their thought patterns, processes, and decision-making techniques. Our interactions with young people must be authentic, demonstrative of respect and value for the youth culture, and we must listen and be open to learning.

Although I have seen and been in situations where sense was not common, I always vow to be a participant of changing and not one of complaining. However, I have witnessed technology attempt to surpass humanity in homes and classrooms all over the world. I have been exposed to things that do not make total sense, although a nugget might be found in it. I have seen some educators teach near math, whereby young people can receive partial credit for being close to the correct answer. They say you are almost correct if you answer 15 to "what is 4 x 4?" Is   15 less wrong than 23,437? My university students have begun to practice a continuum of this phenomena known as "neartime." How about "Near history?" This way I can tell about Maslow's hierarchy of dogs. Why not "Near English?" The hip-hop culture has already embodied this. What if William Shakespeare said, "To Is or Not To Is" or Rene Descartes said "I think therefore I is?" Although the intent may be to encourage, are we distorting encouragement by accepting near or close?

I am the author and presenter who "keeps it real." I don't tell young people that if they should choose to use drugs, they should use clean needles. I say if you chose to use, then you lose-death. I don't tell young people that if they should decide to sell drugs, they should attempt to not be caught. I say if you sell, then prepare for ....jail. Other words would appropriately fit here.

As I portray in many of my adult presentations that no matter how rough or tough their exterior, young people are truly gentle and sometimes fragile beings on the inside. Although many young people are reluctant to admit it, they all want the adults to provide consistency, limits, structure, and boundaries as they grow.

When I address young people of elementary schools, middle schools, high schools, and universities, I find that the more authentic my knowledge and understanding of popular youth culture, the more effective the discussion in terms of positive and prosocial behaviors. In the process, I excite and inform these young people as a result of using familiar ideologies. Their participation is honest and results in actual help for young people to examine positive living and positive decision-making.

I hope you enjoy this book as much as I enjoyed writing it. Please keep in mind that I am a firm believer that to be effective in a young person's life, we must be reflective in our own. At the end of the chapters, I have left opportunities for self-reflection. Self-reflection is a humbling process. It is essential to find out why you think, say, and do certain things...then better yourself. Self-reflection and self-correction are the highest forms of self-learning and healing.

Before we get started, I'd like to thank all of the schoolchildren and teachers who have continued to inspire me on my travels throughout the United States and abroad. I'd also like to thank my wife, my kids and God for keeping me centered in a world that never stops turning.

Be blessed and be a blessing.

Dr. Adolph "Doc" Brown

Chapter 1

The Wheelbarrow

Most people think of a wheelbarrow as a small, single wheel cart designed to transport heavy loads. The first thing that comes to mind might be a construction worker moving cinder blocks, or perhaps a gardener moving a tall mound of dirt. It has become an important tool throughout history, and is a common sight today in many different settings.

The wheelbarrow is actually one of my favorite metaphors for working with young people. Imagine parents and teachers using a wheelbarrow to carry the often-heavy load of our young people. The "heavy load" I refer to is the young persons' lack of self-esteem, self-concept, and a general feeling that they alone are unable to make a difference in the world.

REAL TALK LESSON #1
Labels are for clothing, not for children

Too often, these young people are condemned with a negative label **defiant, rebellious, challenged or troubled**. Good teachers and parents are able to see the good qualities of these students, but often are too distracted or upset by the bad qualities that they lose focus.

Why are so many young people falling through the cracks in our communities and schools? I blame this mostly on the worst "f" word **fear**.

Everyone seems afraid these days, especially in schools. It is no wonder considering all of the negative images in the media of schools and school age children. A "ladder of fear" is developed that trickles down to all levels of the education system.

It works like this; follow me here and see if it sounds familiar: *Teachers are afraid of principals, principals are afraid of superintendents, superintendents are afraid of school boards, school boards are afraid of parents, parents are afraid of children and children aren't afraid of anybody!*

Too often, it is this cycle of fear that ultimately paralyzes teachers and leads to misguided or ignored young people.

Fear keeps many of these young people from succeeding, and it also paralyzes many adults who could otherwise be part of the solution. This fear leads to bad behavior such as disrespect, hostility and loss of focus that we all recognize in young people. These young people become very defensive toward adults and positive peers, and begin to wear their troubled label as a badge.

We often go wrong as adults in treating these behaviors as "acting out" in the current situation. The truth is that these behaviors are rooted much deeper, often in their feelings of hurt, pain, humility and embarrassment. Adult role models must work to go beyond simple discipline of the moment. This is where the wheelbarrow comes into play.

Imagine yourself on a high platform with a tightrope stretching a hundred feet between you and the next platform. You grip the handles of your wheelbarrow ready to cross the tightrope with your wheelbarrow in front of you. Fear is gripping you, as you think of all the things that could go wrong. Most of all, you fear falling and ultimately, failure.

Now imagine that you have to carry a few of the challenged young people you have in your life across the tightrope with you.

Would they agree to go with you?
Would you take them at all?

You may be saying to yourself that this analogy is impossible, so it is not worth thinking about. But please for a second, reflect on how impossible you see the journey of helping a difficult child achieve success.

Is it that different from crossing the tightrope?

Secondly, as an educator, you must think about who is in your wheelbarrow.

Are certain students excluded because of education level, race or economic level?

If the children in your wheelbarrow look the same in any category, then you need to reconsider your decision to teach. What was the original mission, or calling, that brought you into the education field?

REAL TALK LESSON #2
You can be the change

After answering these questions, and considering who is in your wheelbarrow, you should have a better understanding of yourself as a teacher and some possible areas for personal growth. Then, you will have opened yourself to becoming a true change agent for some very special young people who might have slipped by you in the past.

Notes to Nurture Potential & Inspire Excellence In Young People
-- what I've learned from this chapter and what I will change...

_____

_____

_____

_____

_____

_____

_____

_____

_____

_____

_____

_____

_____

_____

_____

_____

_____

_____

_____

_____

Notes to Nurture Potential & Inspire Excellence In Young People
-- what I've learned from this chapter and what I will change...

_____

_____

_____

_____

_____

_____

_____

_____

_____

_____

_____

_____

_____

_____

_____

_____

_____

_____

_____

_____

_____

_____

_____

Notes to Nurture Potential & Inspire Excellence In Young People
-- what I've learned from this chapter and what I will change...

_____

_____

_____

_____

_____

_____

_____

_____

_____

_____

_____

_____

_____

_____

_____

_____

_____

_____

_____

_____

_____

_____

Chapter 2

Real Talk

Next, I'd like to talk to you about one of my favorite types of student. I know this student well because I once was him. I'm talking about the kind of teen who enters a room wearing a rude, intimidating attitude. These are the students who tell you in every word and non-verbal cue that they care very little about everything you have to say. When you meet with these students' parents, they throw their hands in the air and say, "We just don't know what to do with them!"

It's pretty common in education to refer to these types of kids as "at-risk." And by saying "at-risk," we are really saying "at risk of failure." I take a different approach. I prefer to refer to these students as "at-risk of *success*." You may be thinking again that this approach will not work, but please remember that every interaction we have with students is shaping who they are and who they will eventually become.

The best way I've found to approach at-risk students is by, as the kid's say, "Real Talk." Let's face facts. We live in an adult world that often values politically correct, or polite, speech as the only acceptable means of conversation. By "keeping it real", I am simply encouraging you to have authentic and genuine conversations with young people.

Our students see the world as it is and are often confused or afraid about the things they see. They are just beginning to make sense of the world, and without the proper guidance, they can quickly feel lost or even worse, without hope. You know, as an adult, that the world is full of grit, grime and rough edges. Even if you, yourself, have not experienced many of these things first-hand, you know what I am referring to.

Really, all students would benefit from this real type of honest exchange with adults, but let's continue to focus on at-risk youth for a moment. What are some of the benefits you can expect from Real Talk with your students? I believe Real Talk can lead to better classroom management.

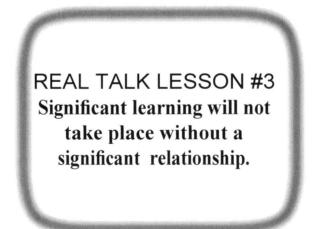

REAL TALK LESSON #3
Significant learning will not take place without a significant relationship.

To be clear, I'm not supporting speaking to students in their own language because that can sound silly or be taken the wrong way from the wrong source; I'm just suggesting you inject more honesty into your conversations. I bet that if you look around at some of the teachers in your building who have best connected with students, this is what you will find.

The following are some of my favorite "Real Talk" statements that I have shared with students and educators across the country:

> **"You cannot learn what you have not read."**
> **"We're involved in education for the outcomes, not the income."**
> **"Wanna Be, Gonna Be!"**
> **"Train your ears, tame your tongue."**
> **"You can and will learn if you come to my class."**
> **"Just because you mess up, does not mean you have to give up."**
> **"You can teach anyone anything, once you have their attention."**
> **"Minimum wage does not self-sufficiency make."**
> **"He said, she said can easily become he dead, she dead."**
> **"Of all the things you wear, your expression is the most important."**
> **"Your classroom is your classroom. Your home is your home."**

And my personal favorite

"If you hit me, please note that I haven't always been an educator, and I know karate, judo, jujitsu and several other dangerous words." (This statement is a combo of humor and firmness, two things that work very well with kids.)

Too often, I fear that young people are frustrated with adults for not telling them the truth about the world. Parents, teachers, and other leaders, do not see the importance that a timely, relevant story could have made in a child's life. The great thing about "Real Talk" is that it will lead to deeper discussions and generally more honest dialogue with students overall.

A dentist friend, who obviously has the chance to talk to many kids in stressful situations, shared with me one of her favorite "Real Talk" statements. When a kid asks her whether they really need to brush their teeth or not, she answers, "Only brush the teeth you want to keep."

Notes to Nurture Potential & Inspire Excellence In Young People
-- what I've learned from this chapter and what I will change...

_____

_____

_____

_____

_____

_____

_____

_____

_____

_____

_____

_____

_____

_____

_____

_____

_____

_____

_____

_____

_____

_____

_____

Notes to Nurture Potential & Inspire Excellence In Young People

-- what I've learned from this chapter and what I will change...

Chapter 3:

Yesterday's School and Today's Students

Hip-hop culture hits harder than either Muhammad Ali or Mark McGuire did, in their heydays. No other trend has evoked as much attention, passion and emotion in modern times. Today's youth see hip-hop as a loud voice of their misunderstood and misinterpreted generation. Although many scholars consider the current concerns about hip-hop to be an overreaction by the older generation, the culture has more grave implications than most want to realize and acknowledge.

For any of you who might feel that this is an "inner city" or "black" issue, please continue reading. The messages of the hip-hop culture are transcending race and ethnicity. If you still don't believe me, take a look at the music charts. Trust me, it's not inner city black youths driving hip-hop to the top of the charts week after week. Who among us has not heard of Fifty Cent or Eminem?

It is truly challenging as an adult to understand the hip-hop generation. This challenge to the older generation has led to a large gap in understanding. One of the major obstacles in bridging this gap in understanding rests with the older generation's lack of knowledge of how to pass the baton of leadership off to the younger generation. The younger generation is reluctant to accept the advice that the older generation has to offer. The worst result of this disconnect is that young people fail to learn the lessons of their parents and other knowledgeable adults like teachers. With the struggles facing the hip-hop culture, it will take the wisdom and guidance of the older generation for today's youth to secure opportunities and overcome challenges.

REAL TALK LESSON #4
**Teach young people that
there is a time and a
place for everything.**

We absolutely need to remind young people that there is a time and a place for everything. Why don't we tell them the truth anymore? I like to share truth all the time with kids. I tell them, "If your mamma still takes you to school, you're not a thug."

Young people want others to accept them as they are. We need to tell them that there is a time and place for everything. There is no reason to speak the Queen's English at all times. There's no need to wear a suit to the beach. But, the ugly truth we need to share is that people will judge our young people based on how they talk, dress and act. The message is that it is okay to have fun and let loose from time to time, but there are also times for seriousness and focus. Please remind them of that for me, will you?

Many critics say the voice of hip-hop is not unlike many voices of protest from prior generations, but it unfortunately carries a very different message from the protest music of Bob Marley or Bob Dylan, for example. I challenge these assumptions, but recognize why this comparison is often made.

Let's look at some of the common themes of the "Hippie" movement from the 1960's:

- •Rebelled against established institutions
- •Criticized middle-class values
- •Opposed the Vietnam War & lost respect for the president
- •Embraced aspects of Non-Judeo-Christian religions
- •Female empowerment, sexual liberation, etc.

For those of you familiar with hip-hop, do you often hear rap music opposing the invasion of Iraq or challenging governmental action? Similarly, while the protest music of the 60s promoted sexual liberation, the lyrics were crafted so that they were not degrading to women. The "Hippie" way was to support gentle protest that supported the ideals of peace, love and personal freedom.

Another major difference of hip-hop culture is the extreme focus on wealth, while also glorifying life on "the streets." Hippies were very focused on not becoming "the Man," a basic archetype of a corporate or government official only out for greed and personal gain. Hip-hop glorifies violence and thug behavior as an acceptable means to attaining wealth. So if anyone, youth or adult, attempts to connect the dots between hippie culture and hip-hop culture, please do them a favor and correct them. Tell them Doc Brown set you straight, and you'd like to help them out.

If you're still not sure about the power of hip-hop culture, visit your nearest mall on the weekend. You will see examples of young people of every race sporting their hip-hop "style." I venture to say this style is on display in most of our schools, whether they are public or private. Well-meaning parents and school officials do their best to keep it out, but hip-hop will always find its way in. In fun, I encourage principals to declare their schools a "No Crack Zone" and outlaw low-hanging baggy pants.

One major part of rap culture is that a performer be "authentic." By this, I mean that they are measured by their knowledge of the streets. This society glorifies many behaviors that are considered unacceptable in civilized life, such as drug dealing, violence and degradation of women. Controversy and criticism of rap culture only seem to make it stronger. In writing this book, I hope to assist in closing the gap between the older generation and younger generation. An important first step in any major change effort is accepting what you do not know.

REAL TALK LESSON #5
**Change is inevitable.
Growth is optional.**

When the gap is not recognized, adults will make up things about a young person, filling in the blanks on their own. Their understanding branches out further from that child's reality and thus widening the gap. For the sake of our young people and our future, we must accept the challenge to grow ourselves. Remember that it is relationships that yield results.

Let's continue.

Notes to Nurture Potential & Inspire Excellence In Young People
-- what I've learned from this chapter and what I will change…

_____

_____

_____

_____

_____

_____

_____

_____

_____

_____

_____

_____

_____

_____

_____

_____

_____

_____

_____

_____

_____

_____

Notes to Nurture Potential & Inspire Excellence In Young People
-- what I've learned from this chapter and what I will change...

Notes to Nurture Potential & Inspire Excellence In Young People
-- what I've learned from this chapter and what I will change...

_____

_____

_____

_____

_____

_____

_____

_____

_____

_____

_____

_____

_____

_____

_____

_____

_____

_____

_____

_____

_____

Chapter 4

Wanna Be, Gonna Be

One of the most controversial figures in hip-hop, and the epitome of the "wanna be, gonna be" philosophy, is Tupac Shakur. Many do not know this, but Tupac was once a truly gifted actor at the Baltimore School for the Arts before his transformation into a "Gangsta." Tupac's former teachers and schoolmates saw no suggestion of the confrontational, belligerent character that eventually dominated his public image. Tupac's zest for learning was evident (in school) as he read books outside under the streetlights because the electricity had been turned off at his home.

Despite being impoverished and raised without a father figure, Tupac experienced great academic success. However, later in Tupac's young adult life, he figured out that he could gain street credibility by getting in trouble with the law. With a combination of his intelligence and street credibility, he became a hugely successful rap star. The criminal charges, as well as street credibility, continued to build: he was shot five times, incarcerated many times, shot two off-duty police officers in Atlanta, was involved in several public fights between his entourage and other rappers' entourages, and charged with sexual assault. As we explore what I call "wanna be, gonna be," Tupac's life story paints a perfect picture to illustrate my point.

Like most young people today, Tupac was vulnerable to the criticism of his peers that he had not paid his dues to be a "real gangster." To add to his oft-publicized violent altercations, he created a swaggering machismo to his character. As young people get obsessed with this life and creating an image, they will enter into a whirlwind of maladaptive activity to show how street-smart they are. Tupac went from one altercation to the next,   always trying to prove how hard or tough, he was.

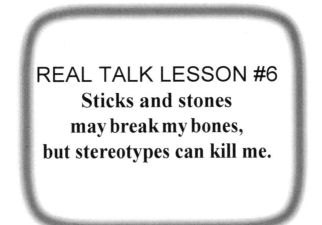

REAL TALK LESSON #6
**Sticks and stones
may break my bones,
but stereotypes can kill me.**

As I often relate to student audiences around the country in reference to my own inner city upbringing, they are surprised to learn that true "gangstas" wish they did not have to live the life they do. Tupac famously had the words "Thug Life" tattooed on his stomach. Most young people do not really understand the loyalties of street culture, especially those of gang culture. Most do not know that Tupac wore red around the Bloods and blue around the Crips.

One of Tupac's most famous feuds was started when he insulted fellow rapper The Notorious B.I.G. by claiming he had had an affair with Biggie's wife. This incident started an East Coast/West Coast war of words, which many became involved in, not having any idea that Tupac had incited the war for publicity. I warn students and educators to use extreme care in the use of "lyrical swords." In short, I like to add "He said, she said," can quickly escalate to "he dead, she dead." Ironically, Tupac and Biggie were murdered. It is worth noting that the artist originally called Puff Daddy not only changed his name, but changed his associations, after the war began. P-Diddy (formerly Puff Daddy) remains alive, very successful, and very well accepted. You may have just purchased one of his designer shirts!

Like everyone, Tupac had a multitude of good and bad qualities. Tupac pushed the limits of the law and human decency, and unfortunately brought an army of followers along with him. The saddest part of Tupac's story is not his tragic death, but instead his years as an intelligent youth, when he was full of potential that was never recognized or realized. Without the guidance of wise mentors, Tupac was left to navigate his young life on his own. Sadly, we know how his story turned out. It is also upsetting to know that Tupac's story is not uncommon among our youths, although he acted his out on a more public stage than most.

REAL TALK LESSON #7
You are only chained down in this life to the extent that you convince yourself you are.

Many of us know of examples of Lesson #7 in our classrooms or in our homes. Perhaps, even you have dealt with these feelings of doubt and lack of self-worth. For those of you who struggle with these issues, I would encourage you to get out of those chains, and get on with the change.

Notes to Nurture Potential & Inspire Excellence In Young People
-- what I've learned from this chapter and what I will change...

Notes to Nurture Potential & Inspire Excellence In Young People

-- what I've learned from this chapter and what I will change…

Chapter 5

The Coach Approach and The Golf Ball

How can a coach ream a player up one side and down the other, yet maintain the player's attention, eye contact, and have them respond with an affirmative, respectful "Yes, ma'am?" The answer is relatively simple. Coaches fully engage their players by bringing their passion, concern and authenticity to their sport. The influence of a great coach on a person's life is phenomenal.

While coaches do face challenges that must be overcome, optimal coaching results in player achievement and success. When coaches get in a rut, they must be courageous enough to try something new. Personally, I like to refer to a "losing streak" as an "opportunity streak." Experimentation is often a tough pill to swallow for a veteran educator with a set routine. But I would argue that by engaging in something new, educators stop focusing on "what isn't working" and begin paying more attention to new behaviors.

REAL TALK LESSON #8
**Success only comes before
work in the dictionary.**

In relation to coaching, the teamwork concept is also a very strong driver of student success. Students are not "achievement machines," and should not be treated as such. As an educator or parent, you know individual students have unique contributions to make. When parents or educators project their own beliefs onto young people, the young person is no longer seen as an individual. Even worse, adults are not able to learn and grow by real interaction with young people. A young person who is valued as an individual is much more likely to be successful and thus want to please elders.

Good coaches do more watching and listening than talking. As a karate instructor and a kickboxing coach, it is just as important for me to believe in my trainee as it is for them to believe in me.

At the center of this belief is my understanding that it is more important for my students to be heard than for me to appear wise.

We begin each class with a mental overview of the preceding day. The class then tackles anything thought which is left unresolved. We collectively listen to that student's concern and then discuss how to learn from that experience.

I remember my own feeling of disconnection from the Zen process when I was a young martial arts student. I asked my Sensei why we began each class with the meditation exercise. He told me he wanted our minds to be clean, clear and calm as the morning river. I told him that I could add a fourth "c-word," chaotic, to his list, if he was describing my brain. Just by listening and valuing my comments, he helped to calm the chatter and chaos of my mind. The more I talked to him, the better I felt. Before long, I found myself showing up early for my class just to sit on the dojo floor and talk to the Sensei about my day. He always listened intently.

As we take a closer look at the "coach approach," as I call it, I'd like to share a concept I like to call the "golf ball method of self evaluation." This method involves the recognition that our personal challenges can be intimidating as well as acknowledging that we can stand improvement in some areas. I call this the golf ball method because it resembles the way that a golf ball is constructed from the inside out. We must identify our own bad habits and replace them with more effective strategies. By choosing to be more authentic with ourselves, we become better suited to recognize our own challenges and opportunities.

REAL TALK LESSON #9
**Be a balcony person,
not a basement person.**

Sigmund Freud explained my golf ball method quite well using the example of "basement versus balcony people." He describes basement people as those who have such a negative outlook that everything in their life appears dismal and unsatisfying. An example of basement people in education would be those on the R.O.A.D. program, or Retirement on Active Duty. Basement people spend much of their time looking for opportunities to be offended. These basement people in an organization are often the drama queens, or drama kings (yes, they're out there too). Unfortunately, teachers who are basement people often spread their negativity and hopelessness to their colleagues as well as to young people.

On the positive side, Freud's balcony people are those who live genuine and authentic lives. Balcony people will typically appreciate the positive elements of their own personalities and the best qualities in others. Balcony people are the personal success coaches who we hear about on a daily basis and who emphatically encourage us to continue our mission. They are the cheerleaders of your organization who are the first ones to applaud each team member's successes. Balcony people in education are those who inspire and nurture the unique talents of each and every student.

We have spoken quite a bit about the difference that teachers can make in a child's life. I want all others who come in daily contact with children to remember the importance of their role. Every football fan knows that a kicker usually sits quietly by as the game goes on. A kicker is almost never featured on TV highlights or has his photo on the front page of the paper. But, think about this how many football games are decided by a play involving the kicker?

REAL TALK LESSON #10
**Every player is important
in a child's life**

A bus driver was one of my best advocates as a child. One driver from my childhood knew that my lights were often turned off at my home, and that I had to deal with other hardships, so she would often pretend to be lost just to give me time to finish my homework on the bus. I truly believe that bus driver knew more about me than many of the social workers that interacted with my family. Whether she was really lost or not is not the issue. What is important is that she took the time and made the effort to care for me. That caring brought me a long way.

By effectively using the coach approach and the golf ball method, any educator will be well on the way to being a person who will have a lasting positive impact on young people's lives inside, outside and long beyond their school years.

Notes to Nurture Potential & Inspire Excellence In Young People
-- what I've learned from this chapter and what I will change...

_____

_____

_____

_____

_____

_____

_____

_____

_____

_____

_____

_____

_____

_____

_____

_____

_____

_____

_____

_____

_____

_____

Notes to Nurture Potential & Inspire Excellence In Young People
-- what I've learned from this chapter and what I will change...

Chapter 6

On a Mission with No Finish Line

"More is always caught than is taught." This should be a parent and educator mantra. The most valuable gifts that we can give to young people are solid role models, a great education and all the love in the world. Young people are always watching us and often looking for gaps between our words and our actions. Young people should be able to examine any educator and see love for every student, passion, creativity and a zest for learning.

I discussed The Coach Approach in the last chapter as an important strategy for educators. Most effective athletic coaches and educators have an intense passion for the game of life, which is often reflected in their players. Good coaches make participation and playing enjoyable while simultaneously teaching important life lessons. When the players master their skills, they reap the benefits throughout their lifetime.

Considering the multitude and complexities of issues faced by today's young people, trust in adults is absolutely necessary for bridges of understanding to be built between young people and adults. Many young people wrestle with issues of loss, abandonment and grief in their lives due to a host of factors including divorce/domestic unrest, mental illness, incarceration and death. The earlier they experience these traumatic events, the less likely the young person will be equipped with the skills and strategies to effectively deal with the trauma.

Many young people develop the defensive styles often displayed by adults to dictate their interactions with teachers, parents and other adults. They resist connecting to adults based on their real, or imagined, fear of experiencing another loss and subsequent period of abandonment. When adults are aware of these behaviors as a symptom of a greater problem, the adult can then respond in meaningful ways to minimize the conflict and form an honest and substantial relationship with that young person.

One of the biggest frustrations for adults is young people's obsession with technology, especially cell phones. Even in the university environment, I encounter the disrespectful actions of students with cell phones and other devices. I have a fun way to get my point across in my classroom though, as I feel they are on my time in my classroom. Feel free to use this in your own classroom.

If a student's phone rings during class, I will ask for the phone and answer it. I will ask who is on the phone and whom they were trying to reach. Then I will tell them that the cell phone owner is busy listening in my class and will have to call them back. Yes, this is a bit of a stunt, but it is one that all of the students in my class will remember. Most of them will do anything to avoid this type of attention. In a fun way, I am teaching them two lessons: to respect elders/teachers and to take their own lives and education seriously. I don't have a great fix for chronic text-messagers, but I'll let you know when I do.

The behavior I mentioned is on public display in the urban style of dress, speech, and behavior within the hip-hop culture. Even adults with a significant amount of training and experience with young people can be guilty of basically standing silently by waiting for a troubled youth to approach them and say, "Excuse me, but could you please help me. I have cognitive dissonance, and I am in need of cognitive-behavioral strategies of intervention."

The young person who wears his pants down past his thighs is communicating his rebellious nature and is almost always lacking a strong male mentor. The young lady who wears her pants as tightly as she can is communicating that she believes she can achieve more attention from the waist down than from the neck up. The young person who wears a black trench coat in 103-degree weather is communicating that they want someone to pay attention to him.

We must listen to the young people to establish meaningful connections with them, as significant learning will not take place without significant relationships. We should not ignore these young people, as it will lead to further alienate them and only increase their feelings of loss and abandonment. When we pretend that certain young people are invisible to us, they internalize this opinion and do not feel bound to the rules and regulations set forth by schools, parents and society-at-large. This dynamic can also open the door to dangerous affiliations with gangs and drug culture.

Educators and parents must both be able to see that "**the tree is in fact in the seed**" when it comes to connecting to today's youth. Every youth, or seed, may or may not have had access to the sunlight, rain or fertile soil of a supportive adult relationship. However, recognition of these facts will lead adults to further understand some of the perils of being a youth in today's world. This is supported by Dr. George Bray's assertion, "Genetics loads the gun, but environment pulls the trigger."

If every adult just attempted to be the sun, rain, or soil for each seed they encountered, more seeds would eventually grow and believe in themselves to say, "I've got a tree inside of me just waiting to grow strong, great and recognizable in this wonderful world. Whatever it may be or wherever it may take me, I am on my way."

Notes to Nurture Potential & Inspire Excellence In Young People
-- what I've learned from this chapter and what I will change...

Notes to Nurture Potential & Inspire Excellence In Young People

-- what I've learned from this chapter and what I will change…

Chapter 7

Keep the Faith, But Not from the Young

As a God-pleasing Christian father, I aspire to teach many lessons to my children. Like most parents, I want to set a good example for my children, provide the best education available and give all the love I can possibly provide. However, among the lessons I deem the most important are what I like to refer to as I.R.S. Independence, Resiliency and Service. I decided that I would tell my children about I.R.S. in an early and positive way.

By teaching independence, I hope to pass on many of the lessons to my children that my mother taught me. As the only male in our home of four women following the divorce of my parents at age 2 and the death of my brother Oscar when I was 11, I recall my mother telling me that she had faith in me. The faith she talked about was more than trust. She told me regularly how much she believed in me, as well as that she expected great things from me and knew without a doubt that I would understand and comply with her rules. To use a flight metaphor, I like to say I received "flying lessons" from my mother and had plenty of teachers to help me "navigate and refuel." I want my children to soar with the same independence.

I strongly desire for my children to be resilient and possess the ability to bounce back from adversity. I want them to know that there is no crime in falling down; the only crime is in not getting up. They need to know that experiencing failure is an integral part of the experience of success. Since life is rather unpredictable and change is the only constant, resilience is in my opinion the most critical aspect to navigating this life.

I have learned to roll with the punches in and out of the ring. No question, it is an absolute requirement to teach young people the value in bouncing back from adversity. I see it as a skill, although many would tell you it is genetic. Remember the quote again, "Genetics loads the gun, but environment pulls the trigger." In my adult home environment, I continually set an example of resiliency by providing examples of personal defeats where I rebounded fiercer than before.

My favorite movie line is from the movie **Antoine Fisher**. When Antoine returns to his former foster home where he experienced emotional, sexual and physical abuse, he makes the statement to his former abusive foster mother,   "I am still standing!" I define intelligence to my children as their ability to adapt and adjust to their environment.

I also love the "comeback kid" mentality of Muhammad Ali, who was once told by a teacher that he "ain't never gonna be nuthin'." In addition to his teacher's use of a double negative, that teacher was apparently very wrong in another way. Young people are often able to rise above challenges, but healthy challenges from parents and teachers can inspire without scarring a young person.

Lastly, I desire for my children to learn to give back. I believe that selfishness is the greatest of all sins. I want them to have a rich toolkit including great interpersonal development, an ability to relate to culturally diverse groups, proper preparation to be productive members of society and a commitment to service now and later. I want them to know that it is difficult to lead if you have never served.

Young people must be given opportunities to shine per the old adage, "Catch them doing good regardless of how small." I often ask my children to identify their accomplishments with the focus on pride, or the good feelings they get about the things they did or qualities they possess. Pride in oneself is very important to a young person's success. Young people are exposed to many conflicting messages, and it takes true effort to quiet these negative forces. Networks like BET and MTV are successful in getting their attention, why can't we?

Even the greatest educational taxonomist Benjamin Bloom agrees that students must "attend" to education before they will "value it." If classroom learning contained the three R's of rigor, relevance and relationships, young people would acquire the three R's of respect for self and others, resiliency in the face of academic challenges and rewards to celebrate as life presents challenges.

To further reinforce the life skill of resilience, adults must be genuine and have the ability to be fallible. A genuine, honest presentation of yourself enables young people to see you as accessible and human.

One word of warning though, do not rely on young people to be your counselor. Often times I have witnessed young parents placing children in positions they do not need to be in. A younger parent will often use the child as a sounding board. Full disclosure of adult realities would be overwhelming to most young minds. That said, allow young people to know that you do indeed make mistakes. Use these mistakes as learning experiences for your children. Once this dynamic, honest relationship is created, you have now created fertile ground for the building blocks of self worth.

As you explore self worth, consider the things that chip away at a young person's self image. Teach the difference between mistakes and bad choices, as we wouldn't want the likes of popular media icons such as Kobe Bryant or Michael Richards to be our children's teachers. Both individuals apologized for their misdeeds by saying they made a "mistake." Hmmm. It is possible both would have been received better if they had said that they had made bad choices and didn't plan on getting caught. If I had the chance to discuss their choices with them, I would share one of my favorite sayings "Character is who you are when no one is watching."

The availability of a good mentor is critical, as all behavior is either learned or allowed. Young people must know that they always have the ability to choose the behavior, but they seldom have the ability to choose their consequences.

Finally, I would recommend developing a family, school or classroom slogan that drives home a message of resilience. On this note, pay attention to any slogans that are regularly repeated by young people. Be sure to reinforce positive statements, and help them to decode the meaning of negative slogans. It's okay to have a little fun creating your slogan. Based on the small stature of the members of the Brown family, we adopted the old adage, "It is not the size of the dog in the fight, it is the size of the fight in the dog" as our family slogan.

Notes to Nurture Potential & Inspire Excellence In Young People
-- what I've learned from this chapter and what I will change...

_____

_____

_____

_____

_____

_____

_____

_____

_____

_____

_____

_____

_____

_____

_____

_____

_____

_____

_____

_____

_____

Notes to Nurture Potential & Inspire Excellence In Young People
-- what I've learned from this chapter and what I will change...

_____

_____

_____

_____

_____

_____

_____

_____

_____

_____

_____

_____

_____

_____

_____

_____

_____

_____

_____

_____

_____

_____

_____

Notes to Nurture Potential & Inspire Excellence In Young People
-- what I've learned from this chapter and what I will change...

_____

_____

_____

_____

_____

_____

_____

_____

_____

_____

_____

_____

_____

_____

_____

_____

_____

_____

_____

_____

Chapter 8

Just the Beginning

The bright side of today's youth culture is again conveyed through the comparison I made in an earlier chapter to hippie culture. As we prepare to begin our mission to help today's young people find success, we need only be reminded that the hippies of the 60's are now set to retire from their white-collar professions. Many hippies who once burned their bras and protested at the Capitol traded in their tie-dye for a suit-and-tie a long time ago.

It is a significant challenge for adults of today to assist the youth culture in learning how to adapt into the professional world. When we accept a viewpoint of the younger generation, we are demonstrating tolerance, not weakness or conformity. With significant relationships harnessing real-life applications and rigorous challenges provided by adults, young people should be capable of performing within some "common sense" boundaries.

Remember that more is "caught than taught," and these boundaries can be shown by adult example, and it should not be a huge problem for young people to express their culture and style through young dress and speech. The mature adult will have surely role modeled that "there is a time and a place for everything," and "high achievement is framed in high expectations."

In summary, although this book is written for balcony adults, don't be misled into thinking that you have to embrace hip-hop as a bridge to young people. We must teach young people how to critically understand and evaluate hip-hop culture as a part of the bigger picture. I'll close with a speech from a very non-hip-hop source. Professional golfer Ben Hogan said he found success by living by ten very important words, "If it is to be, it is up to me."

10 REAL TALK LESSONS

LESSON #1
**Labels are for clothing,
not for children.**

LESSON #2
You can be the change.

LESSON #3
**Significant learning will not take place
without a significant relationship.**

LESSON #4
**Teach children there is a time
and a place for everything.**

Lesson #5
**Change is inevitable.
Growth is optional.**

LESSON #6
**Sticks and stones may break my bones,
but stereotypes can kill me.**

LESSON #7
**You are only chained down in this life
to the extent that you convince yourself you are.**

LESSON 8
**Success only comes before work
in the dictionary.**

LESSON #9
**Be a balcony person,
not a basement person.**

LESSON #10
**Every player is important
in a child's life.**

About the Author

Dr. Adolph "Doc" Brown

 Possessing limitless energy and vitality, Dr. Adolph Brown aka "Doc," is a popular media personality, a noted author, award-winning educator, trained psychologist, columnist, business consultant & coach, sought after motivational speaker, husband, and father of seven. His background as a CEO of The Business & Education Leadership Authority (www.BizEdAuthority.com) brings a wealth of information turned into practical steps for best practices in leadership and learning.

Adolph brings a dynamic and fun approach to each of his customized presentations. You will be informed, inspired and energized with Adolph's creative learning style. He is considered one of the most influential teachers and respected voices of our time in the field of "people," specializing in relationships, achievement motivation, and performance/productivity enhancement. Adolph knows that 'IT' is all about relationships. Whether he is speaking about Real Life Leadership, the fact that Positive Interactions Build Vital Relationships, Trust With Customers or Co-Workers, or the Hope of Our Youth, Adolph knows it starts with a relationship.

Adolph's unique gifts and understanding of human needs have enabled him to reach audiences with life-altering messages. Known for his expertise, humor, down-to-earth speaking style and wisdom, he is a keynote speaker held in high regard. Adolph has been described as a dynamic professional with a high-energy upbeat style and high content intensive delivery. Passion, humor, and audience involvement are key to Adolph's presentations.

Dr. Brown is a Master Teacher, having received international recognition, awards, honors, and distinction in the areas of educational excellence and real-world leadership. He consistently delivers high-quality instruction identifiable by objective audience observers, and makes a significant impact on participant learning gains.

But most importantly, Adolph is real and full of heart. He speaks on subjects and conducts research close to home and is open and courageous about the valleys in his own life and how he has turned his tragedies into triumphs. He has a genuine love for people and a passion for a making a positive difference in the lives of others. He transforms lives daily. Adolph is not interested in touching lives for an hour or two in a presentation but in helping individuals and groups walk away with a lifetime of positive change.

Using his 20+ years experience as a tenured educator, administrator, corporation officer, psychotherapist, trainer and speaker, he will entertain you with his humorous style and wealth of information.

7 Reasons to Book Doc

1. Nationally Recognized Real-World Leadership & Educational Excellence Authority & Master   Teacher
2. Customized Presentations Many Topics Available, All Based On Extensive Research.
3. Workable Solutions Specific to Your Organization
4. Real World Experience Unmatched
5. We Do Not Juggle Offers Plus "No Surprises" Fee Structure.
6. A Seasoned Professional Guaranteed to Make Your Event a Success.
7. Working with Adolph It's Easy! You are the V.I.P., not Doc.

Learn more at www.docspeaks.com

Specialized Keynote Speeches

- Educators & School Counselors
- Colleges & Universities
- Our Children
- Business & Corporations
- Law Professionals
- Marriage & Family
- Mental Wellness
- Faith Communities
- Healthcare
- Real Talk

All presentations available as a single stand-alone, or as one in a two or three part series.

Learn more about scheduling Dr. Brown, future projects and other info @ www.docspeaks.com & www.BizEdAuthority.com

If you like what you read, this is just the beginning. Check in on Doc's other book projects here

www.docspeaks.com/shopdoc/